GW01326341

FROM HALLOWS TO HARVEST

an anthology of the year's turning

Edited by Adam Craig

Published by Cinnamon Press, Meirion House, Glan yr afon,
Tanygrisiau. Blaenau Ffestiniog,Gwynedd, LL41 3SU
www.cinnamonpress.com

ISBN 978-1-78864-058-9

British Library Cataloguing in Publication Data. A CIP record for this book can be obtained from the British Library.

Designed and typeset by Cinnamon Press. Leaping hare adapted from 'hares' © Sergeypykhonin | Dreamstime.com.

Printed in Poland.

Cinnamon Press is represented in the UK by Inpress Ltd www.inpressbooks.co.uk and in Wales by the Welsh Books Council www.cllc.org.uk

Contents

FROM HALLOWS TO HARVEST

All Hallows

(Samhain)

Gabriel Griffin

Ice Age

We have their cold

deep in our bones
their hunger

in the pit of our stomachs

their gods
in the caves of our minds.

Patricia Helen Wooldridge

Walking with Edward Thomas

Something about deeper into woods
sycamore leaves in star bursts
each kissing gate   the past hovering

diagonal light to trodden ground
grass beaded in rain   robin vocals

pools to pick my way through
iron railings in low November halo

weather closing   continuous rain
dove-grey sweeping east   hold onto
this gateway   which feels like home

Donna Kirstein

She comes, waiting to be welcomed

<table>
<tr><td>scent of</td><td>rising mist</td><td>rolling</td><td>north wind</td><td>turning</td></tr>
<tr><td>damp earth</td><td>msasa seeds</td><td>seafogs</td><td>stag's horn</td><td>dropping</td></tr>
<tr><td>blue gum</td><td></td><td>black oak</td><td></td><td></td></tr>
<tr><td>leaves</td><td></td><td>branches</td><td></td><td></td></tr>
<tr><td></td><td></td><td></td><td></td><td></td></tr>
<tr><td>woodsmoke</td><td>clouds of</td><td>crushed</td><td>rime frost</td><td>fleeting</td></tr>
<tr><td>coils</td><td>guti</td><td>shingle</td><td></td><td></td></tr>
</table>

Nigel Hutchinson

At the Year's End

Moon crescent
over morning fields
damp with night dew
at this hour breath hangs
from nostrils — ghosts
of the old year

Donna Kirstein

A November Night

Darkest night
Lonely moon
Lamenting crickets
Carousing clouds

Steady whining
Incessant mosquito
Looming trees
Sudden slap

Deep shadows
Empty garden
Fenced walls
Upturned sky

The pond
centres the sky
drowning stars
in its smooth darkness
but a small splash
ripples out
from my hand.

Distant bark
Damp grass
Creeping dawn
Slow awakening.

Winter Solstice

(yule)

Patricia Helen Wooldridge

Reverie on Thames

Just enough sun to varnish water
shredding the year into diamond cuts

broad   deep   browning   flow
shrinking towards flannelette sky

until   nothing but gleaming mud
someone turned the light on

a redshank's piping flight —

my next life   I will be
lichen   scaling the wind on hawthorn

Ama Bolton

Shortest Day

December
freewheels headlong
through flying leaves
down to the dark hollow
at the bend in the road
a stream to cross
tyres skittering
on thin ice

Nigel Hutchinson

Threshold

Now a shadowy man slips
away with the year's ashes,
casts them into darkness;
dark-haired neighbour arrives
offering a catechism of coal,
bread, salt, luck and life;
greet him with spirits
to soothe his throat, warm
his heart and breathing self.

Derek Sellen

Yule Goat

I butt through gloom,
chewing on tattered leaves
and thin grass beneath snow.

I am the beast of winter,
bearded and lusty,
strong in horn, tooth and gut.

Stripe of black pupil in amber,
my eye is fire,
outshines the frozen moon.

Nigel Hutchinson

Midwinter

Midwinter
cold cloud descends
shallow breathing racks and rattles
frost settles in backbones

CANDLEMAS

(IMBOLC)

Gail Ashton

All this

forgetting
the bud of flame in
your rowan
coltsfoot moon
strewn at its feet
the house

every lit eye fastened to
ribbons
of snow and below
wind-rushed fields
nail tongues
of lark to willow

Patricia Helen Wooldridge

In the Belly of the Woods

The river's full
    and a pliable brown
siskins   wittering   high in the alders

almost in the water   hanging loose
    a clump of snowdrops

to stroll among thousands
    woodland veins on cold breath sky

where the snowdrops have it
    in satin   three petals wide
sprung   in a glance of sun

Nigel Hutchinson

Imbolc

first
lambs:
spring
in
the
air

Spring Equinox

Ama Bolton

Vernal

sleet and fickle sun
and the yells of herring-gulls
wind from the north-east

Sarah Watkinson

Spring Equinox

I live on earth's skin
allowed by leaves.

Some day in March
the ground is firm again —

I could run down the field
to the greening wood.

Grass has pulled water
out of the mud

and sent it away
into the cold wind.

Higher, the white sun
shoots blue into puddles,

lights the apse of the sky.

Steve Xerri

Crossing the Common

Today came the white fire
of blackthorn blossom
catching, suddenly catching

along the hedge in little clusters,
exactly where it flared before:
pale pinholes in folded time.

Vasiliki Albedo

Awrah

I remember lingering
by the window in Riyadh. Tar,
juniper, musk on her neck ripening.
The rush of baring, the rush
of not bearing the black cloth
now heavy on the floor
as we imagined entering the capital
through a window that was just
another opening, to feel the world
clean on our lips, so
familiar in the sun.

Karen Robbie

Daffodil

I glimpse
our vulnerability
as you begin to fade
a folded stem
a withered head
no longer bright
how brief this passing

May Day

(Beltane)

Kathy Miles

Changing the Duvet

He will not fold away this year. Too used
to that sprawl across the bed, plumped-up,
smirking in his own fat belly, and now
this Winter King fights back as you stuff him,
flustered, into the dark blue bag. I hear
a sigh as I handfast his successor
to summer cotton sprigged with columbines.

Fiona Owen

Blue Beltane

Forget-me-nots. Their leaping fireburst.
Theirs is the blue
                                        of multitudes,
of come-again, come-again.
They kindle borders, edges, gaps, cracks —

seeds that try for fertile ground
and find it.

They're hazing May Day, like revelers
kept too long in the dark.

Rachel Spence

Hortus Conclusus

I forgot you for the winter,
turned your face to the wall,
closed the book on your gaze.
You, who had already turned.
You, of the shuttered gaze.
The city gloved in absence,
the river's green sucked back
to its navel of longing.

Today, I blow out my candle,
sleep by an open window,
my collarbones grow flirtatious.
Let's retreat.

Rebecca Gethin

Safe-keeping

When the seeds are sown there's the waiting,
your eyes search the soil for the slip

of a shoot; when grass greens up,
you herd sheep, cows, and horses

to the shieling so that udders
may swell and the young grow on; when,

having kindled the *Beal-tain* and feasted
and drunk all together, each of you

carries a burning turf in your hands
to the hearth; when you circle your home

three times, the sparks writing your place
into the dark, as the trail of flung ash

blesses the earth; when you re-light your fire,
you never extinguish it, smooring the embers

each night, raking the *Tulan nan Tri* with a charm,
you know you've done as much as you can.

Gail Ashton

you are become

a hearth-felt word
moon delirious on a yard
hawthorn
firethorn hand-
fast to sky
night fly
smoke horses in a field
yield of barley
alphabet of flame
bonfire   beltane
consternation
greenwood   ruin
revelation in the rowan

Kathy Miles

Queen

She had wintered the way she knew,
alone in her sepulchre of soil, and it was light

that called her out, bright as a bale-fire,
the slackening of roots in that cold April.

All those months she had drunk sleep
deep as mead, and now fuzzy with waking

she stuttered from the hollowing
she had made like her mother before her,

too drowsy yet for flight. But then the scent
of hawthorn came rushing in, she felt

the unlocking of tulip and primrose,
and her wings latched open, lifted her,

knew their own way to those brimming
hearts where she fretted round the petals.

And later, when night whipped the landscape
into his wide sleeves, pulled a leash of foxes

from his dark magician's hat, she heard
a blether of rooks from the wood,

the jangle of stars above, a crackle
of bonfires on the quickening earth.

Gail Ashton

Be

Eternal riotous a constellation

Lyrical silver what shall I give?

Trees greenwood caught on sky

And fire bright a charm

Now shall I

Earth?

Summer Solstice

(midsummer's day)

Nicola Warwick

Longest Day

Seemed the night
would never come

we ached for the dark,
watched the swifts

swirl and twist
like midsummer dreams

blackbird still sang
late into the evening

heralding the rising
of the moon

Nigel Hutchinson

midsummer

unbounded
hisbreathinhers herswithhis rising
                                                                      falling
playandforeplay playandafterplay
condensednight briefasadream swiftasashadow
enchantedtremblingclock alive
nightshattered starscattered venusbright
onfire thiseveofstjohn

tomorrowabaptism
wildhoney
afeastoflocusts

Patricia Helen Wooldridge

Woodland Tilt

Climb into hanging woods
lean   over   the canopy

summer is a glass of water
showing nothing but a silver skin

remember the small but magnificent waterfall
in midwinter crescendo —

please   keep on falling

By July think only   hydrangea
bubbling cumulus   flirting with land

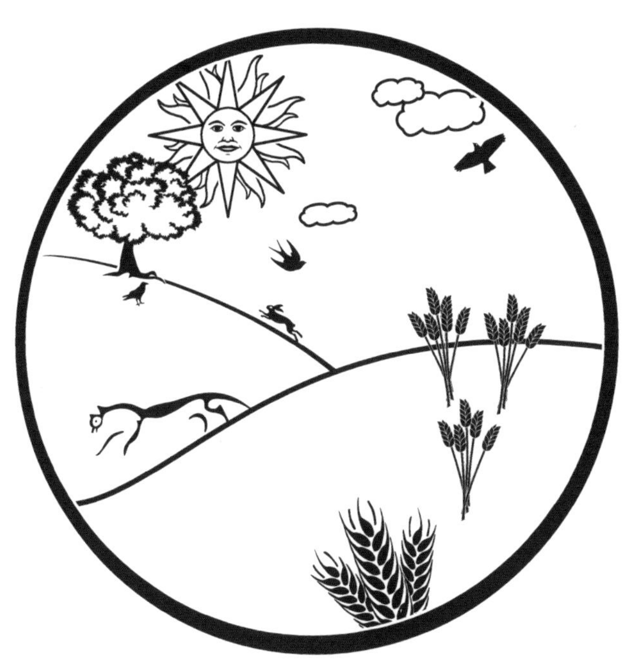

LAMMAS

(HARVEST FESTIVAL)

Fiona Owen

Last of Summer

Bees among a sprawl of lavender —
summer is almost spent, the sycamores
tuned to the shift.
                                        Leaves fray, tatty
from what a lifetime brings; some
already littering the grass, signs
that autumn is underway, that pull
inwards after extroversion.

By the low stone wall,
lemon balm

its scent
hazy —

Ali Jones

Loaf Mass

I have plucked the wheat from the earth
to scent its ancient roots, walked the linescape
between fields, where the land turns over

and comes home to itself in a flurry of dust.
I have learnt how the harvest is a death,
starlings and gulls circle for days,

as worms ghost to the surface
to praise the summer rain.
I know my place. Bats hunt, a night calligraphy,

the smell of changing leaves, the yellow around
the edges that gradually bleeds in.
Home is here, under a low moon, beyond it

other versions of me, travelling onwards
in their own times. I stoop and breathe into
my wine blood, pour it to the soil.

Patricia Helen Wooldridge

There was talk of summer…

What should have been a glut
of raspberries   bleeds

rain-lashed trees   hydra heads
swimming in a green tide
potatoes   too sodden   to lift

I rinse out my pen
note   plump sloes   in July
the colour of ink

begin as if there were
no beginning   August deleted

Nigel Hutchinson

Consider Constable

Consider Constable's quintessential tea towel England
national iconography tourist draw

Ignore Willy Lott's cottage carters clouds
dog ducks   Haywain

Consider midground fields of wheat
peasantry scything swathes to harvest home

Notice this Lammastide labour
urgency of safely gathering in

Consider corn laws rick-burning riots
landless destitution loaf-mass supplicants
earning only crusts crumbs of comfort

Fiona Owen

Lammas

As the year shifts there's yellow
          strip on the greenfinch wing, hypericum
by the rowan mass of starry

flowers, yolk-yellow
and
          evening primroses
          self-seeded lemony, suited
          to tissue-soft petals that sing
of here-then-gone.

All
          this in the high noon heat
of a harvesting sun.

Autumn Equinox

Nigel Hutchinson

Several Roofs Away

that strange sweet smell
of willow leaving summer

rising water floating
narrow weeping boats
downstream

sun rising over there now
several roofs away from
summer

M. J. Oliver

Autumn downpour

Autumn downpour;
Wet with memories
I fly back to the island.

Lapwings too take off in a rush —
A pair of sandals
Still on the shoreline.

Olivia Walwyn

Autumn Equinox

Watches me pat
terracotta tiles, make porridge.

Gets the radiators to regurgitate
old dreams. Has me write

'as if one heart with two
respective halves...' Lies

perfectly horizontal.

Lifts its shadow. I feel
I'm in the balance, somehow.

David Olsen

Equinox

Serrated cherry leaves ignite
their slow curling burn.
In summer you secured gains.
My day is balanced by night.
The keen blade of the wind
will soon rip golden leaves
from every branch, to cower
against the garden wall,
and moulder to blackened dust.
Our tree, bared to its bones,
will bear the winter, trusting
other summers will come.

Chris Considine

Elder

A twisted trunk
and six gnarled stumps
for branches, yet
the tree bears bright green leaves
and berries full of blood.

In my autumnal equinox
can I bear wine-dark fruit?
Next spring
shall I put out fresh leaves
and discs of starry blossom?

Fiona Owen

Equinox

Sudden flap of crows' wings,
leaving. All month, this grit
in my shoe, bruising. Rain's
come, it's dim all day
after perpetual sun's fame.

The year hangs in balance
before its slow slide, breeze
easing the spent to loosen
their summary grip. It's
roots' time, their long thirst
quenched, and mine.